Published in the United States of America by Cherry Lake Publishing
Ann Arbor, Michigan
www.cherrylakepublishing.com

Content Adviser: Cynthia Rathinasamy, Master of Public Policy, Concentration in
International Development, Gerald R. Ford School of Public Policy,
The University of Michigan, Ann Arbor, MI
Reading Adviser: Marla Conn, ReadAbility, Inc.

Photo Credits: ©ZanozaRu /Shutterstock Images, cover, 1; ©Brand X Pictures/Thinkstock, 5;
©U.S. Army Corps of Engineers /http://www.flickr.com/CC-BY-2.0, 7; ©ICRC/Muhammad,
N./www.icrc.org/http://www.flickr.com/CC-BY-SA 2.0, 9; ©duncan1890/iStock, 11;
©Library of Congress, LC-DIG-fsa-8e09007, 13; ©NASA/GSFC/Rebecca Roth/
http://www.flickr.com/CC-BY-2.0, 15; ©Picsfive/Thinkstock, 17; ©Department of
Foreign Affairs and Trade/http://www.flickr.com/CC-BY-2.0, 19; ©Greater Carolinas
Red Cross /http://www.flickr.com/CC-BY-2.0, 21

LIBRARY OF CONGRESS CATALOGING-IN-PUBLICATION DATA
Marsico, Katie, 1980-
  The Red Cross / by Katie Marsico.
      pages cm — (Community connections)
  Includes bibliographical references and index.
  ISBN 978-1-63188-028-5 (hardcover) — ISBN 978-1-63188-114-5 (pdf) —
ISBN 978-1-63188-071-1 (pbk.) — ISBN 978-1-63188-157-2 (ebook)
  1. Red Cross and Red Crescent–Juvenile literature. 2. American Red Cross–Juvenile
literature. 3. Disaster relief–Juvenile literature. I. Title.
  HV568.M26 2015
  361.7'634—dc23   2014006059

Cherry Lake Publishing would like to acknowledge the
work of The Partnership for 21st Century Skills.Please
visit www.p21.org for more information.

Printed in the United States of America
Corporate Graphics Inc.

Note to Reader: Both the Canadian Red Cross and the American
Red Cross are members of the International Federation of
Red Cross and Red Crescent Societies.

THE RED CROSS

CONTENTS

HOW DO THEY HELP?

COMFORT IN A COLD WORLD

A December ice storm knocks out power in Toronto, Ontario. It leaves hundreds of thousands of homes and businesses dark and cold. This is dangerous for people who are old, sick, or caring for small children.

Fortunately, the Red Cross can help. This group serves hot food at local shelters. It helps those

People who need help can go to a Red Cross shelter for a free meal.

What would life be like if you were without power for more than a few days? Furnaces and air conditioners both use electricity. So do microwaves, televisions, computers, and phones.

who had to leave their homes stay safe and warm until the power returns.

Its members help communities struggling with both natural and man-made disasters. They help people affected by storms, floods, fires, earthquakes, and war. The group also encourages communities to grow and develop. It works with residents to improve everything from health care to **sanitation**.

The Red Cross can help rebuild a neighborhood after a storm destroys it.

Are you able to guess how many people the Red Cross helps? Think big! It offers aid to about 150 million men, women, and children around the world.

This international organization supports programs that respect and include people of all different backgrounds and beliefs. It is firmly against **discrimination** and violence.

The Red Cross is interested in helping as many people as possible. They don't favor one group over another. This is true even when two nations or several groups are at war.

The Red Cross goes wherever people need help.

Head to your local library or log on to the Internet. Look for pictures of the Red Cross. What kind of work do you see volunteers doing? How are they helping in communities around the world?

GENEVE

ICRC

DON01PK/PES/10/00091

Split Chana Dal

25 Kg Net Weight

Crop 2009 /10

Pakistan

FROM 1863 ONWARD

Swiss businessman Henry Dunant developed the first Red Cross. In 1859, Dunant was in Italy. A war was going on there. Dunant gathered local residents together. He called on them to give the soldiers comfort and medical attention.

Afterward, Dunant suggested setting up a national organization.

Soldiers on all sides of every war need medical treatment.

THINK!

Think about why it's helpful for Red Cross societies to be neutral. What if they weren't? Do you think it would change how these groups give aid during a war?

11

He wanted people to be prepared to care for the wounded during a war.

Volunteers eventually learned to help communities dealing with natural disasters and **outbreaks** of illness, too.

Soon, other countries began developing similar groups. Great Britain, France, Italy, Japan, and the United States joined together into one international group.

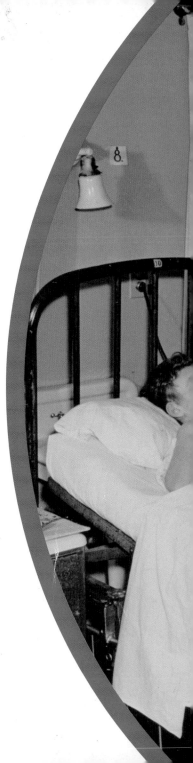

Red Cross workers helped people wounded in World War II (1939–1945).

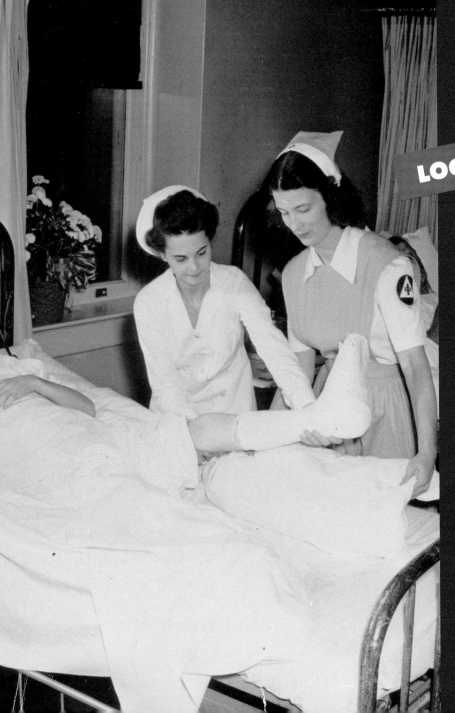

LOOK!

This photo shows Red Cross workers in 1944. Compare what you see to photos of today's Red Cross workers. What differences do you notice?

13

Today, nearly every nation has a Red Cross organization. Some countries call it the Red Crescent Society.

This organization mainly depends on the efforts of its 13 million volunteers. The volunteers teach first aid, act as **translators**, and provide food and shelter to disaster victims.

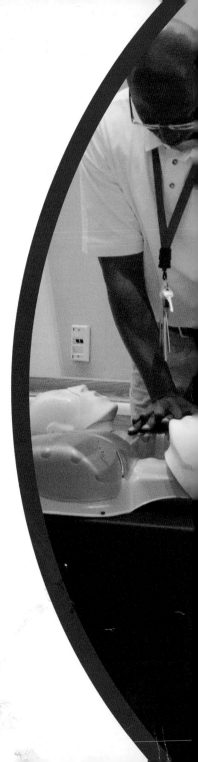

People take Red Cross classes to learn basic first aid.

These volunteers are practicing CPR. Ask an adult to help you find out what CPR involves.

15

EFFORTS THAT IMPROVE LIVES

There are many ways that the Red Cross helps communities prepare for and deal with disaster. They organize blood drives. They also provide disaster victims with emergency medical treatment and **counseling**.

Blood drives are one way that people can contribute to the work of the Red Cross.

A blood drive is an event where people come to donate some blood. Try guessing how a blood drive helps prepare a community for disaster.

17

Volunteers pass out food, fresh water, and **hygiene** kits. They run shelters where people are able to rest and recover indoors. The Red Cross helps victims reunite with friends and family, too.

The Red Cross doesn't wait for disaster to strike to build stronger, safer communities. Some volunteers create programs to provide better sanitation and a steady supply of food and fresh water. Others educate the public

The International Federation of Red Cross and Red Crescent Societies help around the world.

ASK QUESTIONS!

Ask your parents and teachers what projects the American Red Cross and the Canadian Red Cross are currently involved in. These volunteers often help in other countries.

about **vaccinations** and stopping the spread of disease.

Society members also hold workshops and community meetings to help end violence and discrimination.

Thanks to the Red Cross, people in America, Canada, and beyond are able to recover from disaster.

When a disaster strikes a community, the Red Cross will go there as fast as they can.

CREATE!

Create a list of ways you and your classmates and friends could help to support the Red Cross. Perhaps your school could host a bake sale or yard sale to raise money to help others.

21

GLOSSARY

counseling (KAUNT-suhl-ing) guidance and advice that support emotional health

discrimination (dis-krih-muh-NAY-shuhn) the act of treating a person or group unfairly because of their beliefs, background, or physical differences

hygiene (HYE-jeen) keeping yourself and the things around you clean, in order to stay healthy

neutral (NOO-truhl) impartial or unwilling to take sides in a conflict

outbreaks (OUT-brayks) sudden beginnings of something unpleasant

sanitation (sah-nuh-TAY-shuhn) conditions related to public health

translators (TRANTS-layt-uhrz) people who express speech or text in a different language

vaccinations (vak-suh-NAY-shuhnz) shots or drops taken by mouth that protect people against various diseases

FIND OUT MORE

BOOKS

Connolly, Sean. *The International Red Cross.* Mankato, MN: Smart Apple Media, 2009.

Hunter, Nick. *Disaster Relief.* Chicago: Heinemann Library, 2012.

Wade, Mary Dodson. *Amazing Civil War Nurse Clara Barton.* Berkeley Heights, NJ: Enslow Publishers, 2010.

WEB SITES

American Red Cross—Mobilizing the Power of Youth
www.redcross.org/support/volunteer/young-humanitarians
Visit this Web site to find out how kids support the American Red Cross.

Canadian Red Cross—Red Cross Youth
www.redcross.ca/what-we-do/red-cross-youth
Review this Web page for videos and stories about how kids share their time and effort with the Canadian Red Cross.

INDEX

ABOUT THE AUTHOR

Katie Marsico is the author of more than 150 children's books. She lives in a suburb of Chicago, Illinois, with her husband and children.